Silent Triumphs

A journey of Hope and strength

Jyoti Narula Bahl

Made with ❤ on the BookLeaf Publishing Platform
www.bookleafpub.in
www.bookleafpub.com

Dedication

With folded hands and a heart full of devotion, I humbly dedicate this book to my Satgurudev, Shri Shri 108 Shri Madan Mohan Harmilapi Ji—the guiding light of my life. His divine wisdom has been the beacon that has illuminated my path through every storm. His unconditional love and teachings have nurtured my soul, giving me the strength to rise after every fall, the courage to embrace life with faith, and the vision to see beyond challenges. Every verse in this book is woven with the inspiration I have drawn from his grace. It is his blessings that have given me the words to express the beauty of hope, the resilience of the human spirit and the endless possibilities that await those who dare to believe. With utmost reverence, gratitude and surrender at his divine feet.

Jyoti Narula Bahl

Preface

Life is a journey of trials and triumphs, of darkness and light, of despair and hope. Each one of us faces moments when the road ahead seems uncertain, when dreams feel distant and when challenges appear insurmountable. Yet, within us lies an unyielding strength—an ember of hope that refuses to be extinguished.

"Silent Triumphs - A Journey of Hope and strength" is a reflection of this resilience, a testament to the unwavering spirit that rises even after the fiercest storms. Through the verses in this book, I have sought to capture the essence of perseverance, self-belief and the magic of new beginnings. These poems are not just words; they are echoes of countless hearts that have battled adversity and emerged stronger, wiser and more determined.

This book is for the dreamers who refuse to give up, for the warriors who fight silent battles and for the seekers who believe that even the smallest ray of light can illuminate the darkest of nights. It is a companion for those who need reassurance, a reminder that no struggle is endless and no effort goes in vain.

I hope that as you turn these pages, you find comfort in knowing that you are never alone. May these words rekindle your faith, uplift your spirit, and remind you that no matter what life brings—you will win.

With love and hope,
Jyoti Narula Bahl
 bahl.h.jyoti@gmail.com

Acknowledgements

Gratitude is the purest expression of the heart, and as I pen down these words, my heart overflows with thankfulness for every soul, every moment and every blessing that has shaped this journey.

First and foremost, I bow in deep reverence to my Satgurudev, Shri Madan Mohan Harmilapi Ji, whose divine presence has been the guiding light of my life. His wisdom has illuminated my path, his teachings have instilled strength in my soul and his blessings have given me the courage to weave these words. Without his grace, this book would have remained just a dream.

I extend my heartfelt gratitude to my family, whose love and unwavering support have been my greatest strength. Their belief in me has been the wind beneath my wings, encouraging me to continue even when the road seemed uncertain. Their silent sacrifices, their endless patience and their unconditional love have been my anchor in life's storms.

To my readers—you are the true essence of this book. Every word written here is meant to reach your heart, to offer you comfort in times of despair, strength in moments of doubt and the hope that fuels new beginnings. If even a single poem touches your soul and rekindles the light of faith within you, then my purpose has been fulfilled.

Lastly, I express my gratitude to life itself—the countless experiences, the trials that shaped me, the joys that uplifted me and the unseen hands of the universe that have gently guided me toward this moment.

With a heart full of love and gratitude,
Jyoti Narula Bahl

The Road Was Tough, But I Kept Walking

The road was tough, with stones that stung,
A journey unknown, with no songs sung.
Each step I took, was heavier than before,
But I kept walking, my heart wanting more.

The winds were harsh, the sky never clear,
I stumbled, I fell, but still, I drew near.
For with each fall, I found my rise,
I learned to embrace the strength in my cries.

The road was long, but my spirit never swayed,
Every bruise, every tear and every price I paid.
For the road that was tough, led me to light,
And now I stand strong, with my heart burning bright.

The journey, once weary, now feels so sweet,
For in every struggle, I found my feat.
The road was tough, but I kept moving on,
And in that perseverance, I became reborn.

Give Your Dreams Wings to Fly

Dreams are whispers, soft and sweet,
They flutter in the heart's quiet beat.
Like birds waiting for the wind to rise,
Dreams take flight under open skies.

Give your dreams wings, let them soar,
Beyond the boundaries, forever more.
In the silence of doubt, let them sing,
With every flutter, they'll take wing.

Do not cage them in fear or regret,
For dreams are the treasures you haven't met.
They will guide you, if you dare to see,
A world beyond what is and what can be.

So give your dreams wings, let them fly,
Let them paint your canvas, let them touch the sky.
For in those wings, your future will be,
A masterpiece waiting for the world to see.

Victory Belongs to Those Who Never Quit

Victory is a distant goal,
A treasure sought by a restless soul.
The journey is long, the path unclear,
But those who persist, will find it near.

In the face of failure, when hope seems lost,
Those who endure, no matter the cost,
They rise again, with a heart so true,
For victory belongs to the brave few.

Each step is a battle, each breath a fight,
But every challenge is worth the sight.
It's not the fall but the courage to stand,
That turns the dust into victory's land.

So when the road is rough and skies are grey,
Remember, success is just a step away.
For victory belongs to those who never quit,
And in that persistence, their dreams will fit.

Today Is the Most Precious Gift

Today is a gift, wrapped in light,
A treasure that shines so pure and bright.
It holds no regrets, no yesterday's pain,
Just the promise of joy in every gain.

Yesterday's gone, tomorrow's unknown,
But today is a seed that we've all grown.
In its hours, there's a chance to be,
The best version of you, the best version of me.

Today holds the moments we often forget,
The laughter, the smiles, the quiet sunset.
It's a pause in time, a peaceful sigh,
A chance to spread wings and learn to fly.

So embrace today and make it count,
For in its moments, life truly amounts.
Tomorrow will come but don't forget,
Today is the most precious gift yet.

A Smile Can Change the World

A smile is a ripple, soft and kind,
It touches hearts, it eases the mind.
Like sunlight breaking through the rain,
It calms the storms, it soothes the pain.

A smile is a gift, simple and pure,
A cure for hearts that aren't sure.
It's a bridge between two souls apart,
A language of love, a work of art.

In the darkest times, a smile can shine,
A beacon of hope, a light divine.
For in that curve, there's a world of grace,
And a new dawn, a brighter place.

So give a smile, share it wide,
Let it spread far, let it be your guide.
For a smile can change the world, you'll see,
A simple act of kindness, for you and me

What You Have Is More Than Enough

What you have is more than enough,
It's the quiet strength when life gets tough.
In the simplest things, there's beauty untold,
In the warmth of home, in the love you hold.

It's not in the riches, nor in the fame,
But in the quiet moments, free of shame.
It's the laughter shared with friends so dear,
And the peace you find when you draw near.

What you have is more than enough,
It's the courage to love, the strength to be tough.
It's in the small joys, the little things,
The way your heart dances when it sings.

So count your blessings, hold them tight,
For in your hands is all that's right.
What you have is more than enough,
A heart full of love, a life that's tough.

.

No Matter How Dark the Night, Dawn Always Comes

The night may be long, the stars may hide,
But deep in the darkness, there's hope inside.
The moon may fade, the winds may howl,
But trust in the dawn, it will end the prowl.

For night is but a shadow, fleeting and brief,
A moment of sorrow, a season of grief.
But the sun rises with a golden grace,
Turning the night into a bright embrace.

So hold on tight through the cold and the pain,
Know that dawn will break and peace will reign.
No matter how dark the night may seem,
The light of dawn is more than a dream.

Let your heart be strong, your spirit bold,
For the morning brings warmth like a hand to hold.
In every night, there's a dawn to come,
And in that dawn, we'll find our home

Those Who Rise After Falling Create History

Falling is part of the game we play,
We stumble, we break, we lose our way.
But those who fall are never lost,
For in rising again, they pay the cost.

It's not in the fall but how we stand,
How we rise with hearts unmanned.
The scars we carry, the battles we fight,
Are what make us strong, give us our might.

History is not made by the perfect stride,
But by those who get up after they've cried.
In the face of failure, they find their fight,
And in their rise, they set things right.

So fall if you must but rise with grace,
For history remembers those who embrace
The power of strength that comes from within,
Those who rise after falling — they win

Learn to Trust Yourself

In a world that pulls, that speaks so loud,
It's easy to lose sight, to fall from the crowd.
But deep inside, there's a voice so true,
It whispers, **"Trust yourself and let your heart guide you."**

The world may doubt, it may criticize,
But only you can see through your own eyes.
Trust the dreams that spark inside your chest,
For they know the way to your very best.

The path won't always be clear or wide,
But within you lies the strength to decide.
So listen to that voice and let it guide,
For trusting yourself will turn the tide.

Learn to trust your heart and mind,
For in their wisdom, your strength you'll find.
The world may change, but stay true to you,
And your dreams will come alive in all that you do

Every Effort Counts

Every step you take, though small it seems,
Is a building block for your grandest dreams.
No effort is wasted no task too slight,
Each one brings you closer to the light.

In moments of doubt, when progress feels slow,
Remember the seeds you've yet to sow.
Every effort, every moment you try,
Brings you closer to reaching the sky.

It's neither about speed nor how fast you race,
But the determination you hold in place.
Every effort, whether big or small,
Contributes to your growth, to your rise, to it all.

So keep pushing forward with every chance,
For every effort is part of your dance.
And in the end, when you look around,
You'll see every effort has made you profound.

Never Give Up

In the face of doubt, when the road is steep,
When your heart is heavy and you can't sleep,
Never give up, never lose sight,
For the darkest hour brings the brightest light.

The path may twist, the winds may howl,
But your heart is stronger than any foul.
When your spirit falters, hold on tight,
For the dawn is closer, just out of sight.

Never give up, though the journey is long,
Every step you take makes you strong.
The storms will pass, the clouds will clear,
And you'll find the strength that's always near.

So keep going forward, no matter the fight,
For in the end, you'll reach the light.
Never give up, for hope is alive,
And with each new breath, you'll thrive

.

Rise Up, Stand Tall

Rise up, stand tall and face the day,
Let your heart lead, let it find the way.
The world may try to knock you down,
But you're made of strength, wear it like a crown.

Stand tall like the trees that touch the sky,
For you were born to soar, not to shy.
Every struggle you've faced, every tear you've shed,
Has made you stronger, its part of your thread.

Rise up, when the world says no,
Let your dreams and courage grow.
Stand tall, like the mountains so grand,
For you are capable, take a stand.

Embrace your power, your voice, your fight,
For in your rise, you'll find the light.
Stand tall, and let the world see,
That nothing can stop the strength in me.

Meeting Myself Again

I searched for myself in a thousand faces,
In places bright and dark.
In echoes of laughter, in silent spaces,
In every fading spark.

I chased the dreams the world had set,
Yet lost my soul on the way.
I wore a mask to please them all,
While my heart began to fray.

One day, the mirror spoke to me,
Not of success or gain.
But of the child I left behind,
The one who danced in rain.

I met myself in quiet moments,
When no one else was near.
In unchained thoughts, in fearless hopes,
In the voice I failed to hear

I am not the fears they gave me,
Not the doubts they made me hold.
I am the fire, the dreamer's light,
The story yet untold.

So here I stand, no mask, no chains,
With open heart and eyes.
I've met myself, I know my name,
And I refuse disguise

The Strength Unseen

Not every victory makes a sound,
Not every battle leaves a scar.
Some rise like the morning sun,
Softly shining from afar.

The mother who never complains,
Though her heart is heavy with pain.
The father who walks the extra mile,
So his child may never strain.

The dreamer who never gives up,
Even when mocked by the crowd.
The artist who paints in silence,
But never seeks to be proud.

These warriors don't seek applause,
Nor do they long for fame.
For they know that true success,
Is not just in name.

They carry their struggles alone,
With a quiet, unshaken grace,
And though the world may not notice,
They have already won the race.

Whispers of Victory

No trumpets sound, no banners rise,
Yet victories happen in silent skies.
A woman stands after a stormy night,
With steady hands and newfound light.

A student burns the midnight flame,
Chasing knowledge, defying shame.
A heart forgives without a plea,
Setting its wounded soul free.

The seeds of hope are sown alone,
Where no one sees, where none have known.
Patience waters, time makes it grow,
And suddenly, their light will show.

For triumph isn't always loud,
It isn't found in a cheering crowd.
It's in the moments no one sees,
In the silent strength, the quiet pleas.

So hold your ground, walk your way,
Success will find you, come what may.

Unheard Applause

Who celebrates the battles won.
In silence, behind closed doors,
Who sings for those who stand alone.
On life's uncertain shores.

The single mother, working late,
Who hides her struggles well.
The elder with a trembling hand,
Who still has stories to tell.

The child who dares to dream so big,
Despite a world unkind.
The poet who writes in midnight's hush,
Yet keeps their words confined.

These triumphs don't demand the stage,
They bloom where none can see.
For strength is built in quiet ways,
And whispers hold the key.

So though the world may never hear,
The battles that you've crossed,
Know that victory isn't lost,
It's
just... an unheard applause

Rising in Silence

They said she'd fail, she wouldn't last,
That she was just a dreamer.
Yet there she stood, against the storm,
A quiet, fearless schemer.

He worked alone, he burned the night,
His efforts went unseen.
But what they missed, what they ignored,
Would shape the world's new dream.

The silent rise, the humble soar,
Beyond the reach of sight,
For sometimes strength is never loud,
Yet glows with endless light.

No need for praise, no need for fame,
No stage, no grand ovation.
For those who rise despite the odds,
Are walking inspiration.

The Quiet Champions

Some dreams are built with silent hands,
Some struggles go untold.
Some heroes shine without the light,
But their hearts are purest gold.

A teacher stays beyond the bell,
For the child left behind.
A doctor holds a trembling hand,
With patience, calm, and kind.

A friend who listens, without words,
When the world turns away.
A soul who prays for someone else,
As night dissolves to day.

Not all who win seek victory's glare,
Not all who rise need fame.
But silent champions walk among us,
And life is never the same

Turning the Page of an Unfinished Story

The story's not over, it's just begun,
The battles you face, the wars you've won.
Each page is a lesson, each word a scar,
But your story is yours, and you're the star.

So turn the page, and start anew,
A chapter of hope, a chapter of you.
The past is a whisper, the future is bright,
And every new page will bring its light.

The ink is fresh, the pen is in hand,
Your story is yours, to understand.
Don't let the past write the next line,
For the power of your story is truly divine.

So turn the page and let it be told,
Your story is magic, it's worth its gold.
Each page you turn, brings you closer to free,
For your unfinished story is your destiny.